The Princeton Review

Job Notes:

Resumes

The Princeton Review

Job Notes:
Resumes

BY TIM HAFT

Random House, Inc.
New York 1999
www.randomhouse.com/princetonreview

Princeton Review Publishing, L.L.C.
2315 Broadway, 2nd Floor
New York, NY 10024
e-mail: comments@review.com

ISBN 0-679-77872-1

Editor: Amy E. Zavatto
Designer: Illeny Maaza
Production Editor: Bruno Blumenfeld

Manufactured in the United States of America on partially
recycled paper.

9 8 7 6 5

Acknowledgments

First and foremost I'd like to express my gratitude to the thousands of clients I've worked with over the years—you've taught me a great deal about life, work, and writing resumes. Thanks to my editor, Amy Zavatto for her skillful handling of my sometimes not-so-skillful prose, and to Illeny Maaza and Greta Englert for making the book look so good. A big high-five goes to my colleagues Michelle, Marci, and Meg for hanging tough and never saying die. A special thank you to my partner Audrey who helped me keep it all in perspective even when the chips were down. And thanks to my family and friends for believing in me and bailing me out when I needed help.

Contents

What's a Resume?

A resume is a carefully tailored marketing tool that summarizes one's employment qualifications for a pre-defined target audience. In other words, it's the calling card that you're going to present to your future boss. In some respects a resume is similar to a print advertisement, only in this case the product is you and the consumer is your prospective employer. Unlike many of today's ads, however, a resume's content should be completely factual, results-oriented, accurate, and honest. The focus should be on verifiable accomplishments and skills, rather than on subjective qualities such as attitudes or personality traits. Employers want to know in concrete terms what you can do for them tomorrow if they hire you today. The best indication of this is what you've achieved in the past, not whether you're a hard worker or a nice person.

To be effective, a resume should be targeted—either toward a specific job opening, a particular field (e.g., retail management), a person you hope to impress, or a position you wish to create. Whichever target you choose, the goal of your resume is the same—to enable you to meet face to face with the person who has the authority to hire you, or at least elevate you to the next step of the employment process. No resume, no matter how outstanding, will ever land you a job offer—that can only be accomplished through the employment interview. Just because you have a strong resume don't assume that you can sit back and wait for the offers to roll in—they won't. In fact, don't be surprised if you send out over 100 resumes without receiving a single response. Your resume is only one instrument in your job search toolkit, and in a sense it's quite limited. To be a successful job hunter, you must know how to skillfully use all the tools at your disposal.

Although to some extent your resume is a documentation of your past, it also needs to be geared toward your future. It should be making a statement about where you would like to be next, as opposed to where you've already been. Try to avoid creating what resume consultant Yana Parker aptly calls a "career obituary." Also, keep in mind that there's not much sense in stressing skills that make you marketable if you have no desire to use them in the workplace. Discussing what's on your resume during an interview should excite and motivate you, not make you cringe or put you to sleep.

How Long Should My Resume Be?

Your resume should generally be one page in length. However, you may extend it to two pages or more if you have several years of relevant work experience or if you're pursuing a field such as teaching, in which length isn't really an issue. Suffice it to say, however, that if you're looking for a job in a traditional business field such as accounting or banking and you have less than five years of relevant experience, your resume should be no more than one page.

WHAT ON EARTH IS A C.V.?

As a job hunter you may occasionally hear the term *c.v.*, or *curriculum vitae*, particularly in the world of academia. Just because you opted out of Latin in high school, don't let these foreign words intimidate you. The only difference between a resume and a c.v. is that the latter provides more details about an applicant's experience—otherwise, the principles espoused in this book apply equally to both types of documents.

I've got an "in" at this cool company —do I really need a resume?

While you may hear some job search consultants tell you to throw away your resume, we believe that no matter what type of job you're seeking—full-time, temporary, internship, consultancy, fellowship, or whatever—you will undoubtedly benefit from having one. Even if you gain entree to an organization through your good old Uncle Ernie, it will still behoove you to prepare a resume. The fact is that practically all prospective employers will feel more comfortable if they can see your qualifications in print before they speak with you in person. This gives them an opportunity to carefully analyze and digest what it is you are offering, and give some thought as to the types of questions they'd like to ask when they finally meet you. Also, it's no secret that most employers won't remember half of what you say during an interview, so they'll need your resume to serve as a reminder of your key qualifications.

What it boils down to is this: employers (i.e., those who have the power) have decided that the most efficient way to screen out the thousands of applicants who want to get hired (i.e., those who have no power) is to first review their qualifications in a highly condensed form (i.e., the resume) that can be presented on paper or, increasingly, electronically. No employer has the time to speak individually with every person who applies for a job. But with a little help from their assistants and computer systems, they *can* quickly sift through hundreds or even thousands of resumes in short order, thereby whittling down the field of suitable candidates to a manageable number. Your goal is to make it onto that short list and this book will show you how to do just that.

How Do I Get Started?

Before setting pen to paper or fingers to keyboard, you'll avoid many potential headaches if you try your best to answer the following questions:

WHAT TYPE OF WORK WOULD YOU LIKE TO DO?

Are you interested in writing press releases, selling deodorant, researching consumer buying trends, or teaching English in Eastern Europe? Try to focus on the activities that particularly motivate, energize, and interest you. The more specific your answer, the easier it will be for you to compose your resume, since you will have identified the core of your self-marketing pitch (e.g., "I would like to coordinate conferences for a nonprofit health advocacy organization."). Once you're clear on the nature of the work you're seeking, you'll need to research the fields within which this type of work can be done. Identify the specific job titles that tie in with your interests and make a list of what skills are required to excel in those jobs.

Of course, sometimes our lives temporarily necessitate that we find work for purely practical reasons. After all, we need to pay rent, eat a meal every now and then, and put some clothes on our backs. If you're putting together a resume because you need to find a job pronto out of economic necessity, you'll be best served by focusing on your most marketable skills—the ones that will get you hired in a jiffy. You can always pursue your dream job once you're back on your feet and have paid off your credit card debts.

- The activities that I most want to engage in on a daily basis are:

  a)

  b)

  c)

  d)

  e)

WHAT ARE YOUR FIVE GREATEST STRENGTHS/SELLING POINTS THAT RELATE TO YOUR JOB OBJECTIVE?

In other words, why should someone hire you for the position in which you are interested? Try reflecting on your moments of triumph—those times when you were especially proud of what you accomplished. Also ask your closest friends, family members, teachers, and colleagues for their opinions about what you do best. Write down specific examples of how you've used your strengths in the past to achieve verifiable results.

- My five greatest selling points are:

  a)

  b)

  c)

  d)

  e)

WHICH ORGANIZATIONS OFFER THE TYPE OF OPPORTUNITY YOU ARE SEEKING?

To answer this question, you'll need to consult a wide variety of sources including industry directories, the Internet (e.g., search for industry-based chat groups, employment sites, and company profiles), professional associations connected to your field of interest, and trade publications. Start by asking the people you feel closest to if they might be able to direct you to someone in your target field. Industry insiders are likely to have the most accurate and comprehensive information on where the jobs are. Also, check with your high school or college alumni association, and, if you have access to it, your university's career development center. These organizations may be able to put you in touch with fellow alumni who are already working in your field of choice. Don't make the mistake of relying entirely on the help wanted section of the newspaper; the majority of employment opportunities are never even advertised.

The organizations that offer the type of opportunity I'm seeking are:

1.

2.

3.

4.

5.

6.

7.

8.

9.

10.

11.

12.

13.

14.

15.

16.

17.

18.

19.

20.

WHAT DO YOU KNOW ABOUT YOUR PROSPECTIVE EMPLOYERS?

Just having the names of a bunch of companies won't help you write a targeted resume, and without a targeted resume you're putting yourself at a definite disadvantage. It's your job to investigate each organization you plan to approach to gain a sense of the challenges they're currently confronting and how you might be able to help them overcome those challenges. Ideally you want to get right in the head of your prospective employer and figure out what it is he's looking for in an employee. Nine out of ten times he'll be seeking someone to solve his problems, whether they concern selling soda to octogenarians, establishing a shuttle service to the moon, devising a database of health spas, or developing a cure for acne. Your resume must convince the employer that you can solve his problems.

Thorough research will help you tailor your resume so that the qualifications you present on paper closely match the needs of your target employer. This is not to say that you must prepare a separate resume for every single employer—after all, many organizations are virtually indistinguishable from one another and are seeking essentially the same qualities in a candidate. You should, however, at least get into the habit of evaluating every employment situation on a case by case basis and modifying your resume as needed.

Building a Foundation

WARMING UP FOR THE TASK

One of the best ways to get ready to write your own resume is to trash somebody else's—preferably somebody you don't know. It's a fun, risk-free way to learn about what not to do. Fortunately, Miles Goodyear has generously offered up his resume for sacrifice. On the next page is Miles's feeble attempt to put himself on paper. Go ahead, mark it up, tear it to shreds, laugh out loud—don't worry: Miles can't hear you. For each mistake you identify make a mental note about how you would fix it.

Once you've practically used up all the ink in your red pen, take a gander at page 11. Here we've reconstructed Miles's resume to conform with the principles set forth in this book.

How does the revised version mesh with your critique? Were you able to catch most of the formatting, spelling, and content errors? If not, did you at least manage to get rid of some of those aggressive feelings you've been harboring inside? Good. Now let's turn our attention to creating your Qualifications Bank.

Feeble Attempt

MILES GOODYEAR
924 West End • New York, New York 11222

EDUCATION
UNIVERSITY OF MIAMI
B.A. in International Relations
GPA: 2.7
Miami, FL
December 1997

HARVARD UNIVERSITY
Writing courses
Cambridge, MA
Summer 1996

EXPERIENCE
UNIVERSITY OF MIAMI ALUMNI RELATIONS
Development Assistant
Miami, FL
9/96-Present
- Conduct research on potential donors.
- Compile data for annual reports and office library; organize donor information.
- Train and supervise college work-study students.
- Monitor office budget.
- Provide administrative support to the Director of Development and Alumni Research.

UNIVERSITY OF MIAMI
Special Events Manager
Miami, Fl.
9/12/94-5/13/95
- Answered phones, filed and used fax machine.
- Assisted in planning and directing events.

LIMITED EXPRESS
Intern, Public Affairs Department
New York, NY
Summer 1993
- Researched and wrote drafts for press releases.

UNIVERSITY UNION TELEVISION
Student Reporter
Miami, FL
- Collected and organized information and interviewed guests.

CITY YOUTH PAPER
Editor
New York, NY
Summer 1992
- Selected subjects to interview for city-wide, monthly news magazine.
- Scheduled and conducted interviews; wrote articles

VOLUNTEER EXPERIENCE
Soup Kitchen Volunteer. Cooked and fed the homeless in Miami.
Tutor. Provided tutoring for high school student in math and english.
Candy Stripper. Volunteered at St. Luke's Hospital.

SKILLS AND INTERESTS
Languages: Know French
Computers: Proficient on IBM and Macintosh (MacWrite, Microsoft Word, WordPerfect, Lotus 1-2-3, Excel)
Interests: Horror movies, checkers, red Jell-O

References Available Upon Request

Revised

Miles Goodyear   924 West End • New York, New York 11222 • 212—URF-UGLY

Education

December 1997
University Of Miami, Miami, FL
Bachelor of Arts, International Relations
- On-air interviewer for University Union Television.

Summer 1996
Harvard University, Cambridge, MA
- One of twelve students selected through a national essay contest to participate in an eight week workshop on speechwriting.

Experience

1996–Present
University of Miami Alumni Relations, Miami, FL
Development Assistant
- Analyzed the donation potential of recent alumni and presented findings in a ten-page report to the Director of Development.
- In charge of data collection for the annual report.
- Train and supervise six work-studies; conduct work-study employment interviews and make hiring recommendations.
- Utilized Excel to maintain office budget of over $2,000,000.

1994–1995
University Of Miami, Miami, FL
Special Events Manager
- Collaborated with a team of five on the planning and implementation of numerous large-scale special events including the Orange Bowl Parade and Hurricane Relief Concert.

Summer 1993
Limited Express, New York, NY
Intern, Public Affairs Department
- Acquired a solid understanding of the media relations process.
- Wrote press releases and news briefs.

Summer 1992
City Youth Paper, New York, NY
Editor
- Interviewed local politicians for this monthly news magazine (circulation: 32,000).

Community Service

St. Ignatius Soup Kitchen—Served meals to homeless men and women.
P.S. 125—Tutored a high school student in math and English.
St. Luke's Hospital—Assisted nurses on their daily rounds.

Skills

Languages: Conversational French
Computers: Familiar with IBM and Macintosh platforms. Expertise in MacWrite, Microsoft Word, WordPerfect, Lotus 1-2-3, Excel

11

CREATING YOUR QUALIFICATIONS BANK

Writing your resume will be infinitely easier if you first take the time to set up a repository of relevant experiences, skills, accomplishments, and knowledge. By establishing what we call a "Qualifications Bank," you will ensure that you have all the necessary information at your fingertips every time you sit down to compose a new resume or revise an old one. Creating your resume will then be as simple as making an information withdrawal from the Bank and arranging that information in such a way that your most relevant strengths are highlighted.

Fortunately, unlike your neighborhood S&L, your Qualifications Bank will never go bust. In fact, it will constantly grow and expand throughout your life, enabling you to become increasingly selective over time about what you place on your resume.

To create your very own Qualifications Bank just fill out the handy worksheets we've provided on the next few pages. As you go through this process you may also want to enlist the help of some of the people who know you best. Friends, family, co-workers, employers, teachers, and coaches may be able to help you fill in the gaps and remind you of some of the noteworthy experiences that have slipped your mind. For those jobs that you performed while in a semi-comatose state, consider consulting the Dictionary of Occupational Titles (available from your friendly reference librarian), which, although one of the driest books ever created, provides handy descriptions of just about every job title imaginable.

Although you may be tempted to zip through this dramatic and exciting process, in the long run it will be well worth your while to be as thorough and descriptive as possible in completing this task. While much of the information in your Qualifications Bank may not end up on the final draft of your current resume, we can almost guarantee that five years from now, when you are desperately trying to change jobs or transfer into a new field, you'll be glad that you have this information available. It will also prove helpful for filling out employment applications, which often ask for a much more complete history than what's typically provided on a resume. At the very least your Qualifications Bank may come in handy when you begin writing your memoirs.

Graduate School Education

1. Name of institution

   _____

2. Location of institution (City and State)

   _____

3. Dates of attendance

   _____

4. Degree

   _____

5. Thesis/Dissertation topic and description

   _____

   _____

6. Area of study

   _____

7. Research interests

   _____

   _____

8. Overall GPA

   _____

9. Courses completed and grades received

   _____

   _____

   _____

10. Significant projects/papers

   _____

   _____

11. Merit-based scholarships, academic honors, and other school-based honors or awards

_____

_____

College Education

1. Name of institution

_____

2. Location of institution (City and State)

_____

3. Dates of attendance

_____

4. Degree

_____

5. Major(s)

_____

6. Minor

_____

7. Overall GPA

_____

8. Major GPA

_____

9. Class rank

_____

10. Courses completed and grades received

_____

_____

_____

11. Significant Projects/Papers

_____

_____

12. Merit-based scholarships

_____

_____

13. Academic honors such as Dean's List, Phi Beta Kappa, Magna Cum Laude, etc.

_____

_____

14. Other school-based honors or awards

_____

_____

High School Education

1. Name of institution

_____

2. Location of institution (City and State)

_____

3. Dates of attendance

_____

4. Diploma

_____

5. Curriculum

_____

6. Overall GPA

_____

7. Class rank (if known)

_____

8. Courses completed and grades received

_____

_____

_____

9. Merit based scholarships

_____

_____

10. Academic honors

_____

_____

11. Other school-based honors or awards

_____

_____

Additional Training

This is the place to list all the continuing education classes, seminars, and workshops you've attended. Make sure to indicate the title and subject of the class, the name and location of the organization or institution that offered it, the year you attended, and, if applicable, the skills or knowledge you acquired through participating.

1.

2.

3.

4.

5.

6.

7.

8.

9.

10.

Standardized Test Scores

ACT
SAT
GRE
MCAT
LSAT
GMAT
Other Tests

Work Experience

Include paid and volunteer positions, as well as internships

Job #1

1. Name and address of employer

   _____

   _____

2. Description of employer (e.g., type of business, number of employees, etc.)

   _____

3. Job title

   _____

4. Dates of employment (month and year)

   _____

5. Reasons for leaving

   _____

   _____

6. Name and phone number of direct supervisor (will this person be a reference?)

   _____

   _____

7. What were your major accomplishments on the job? (e.g., promotions, awards, special recognition. What did you initiate, create, design, revamp, etc.? How did these accomplishments affect your employer's bottom line?)

_____

_____

_____

8. What were your major job responsibilities? In what types of tasks or activities were you typically engaged?

_____

_____

_____

9. What new knowledge or insights did you gain? (e.g., acquired knowledge of the book proposal review process by sitting in on weekly meetings with the Acquisitions Editor)

_____

_____

_____

10. What skills did you acquire or improve upon? (e.g., became adept at public speaking)

_____

_____

_____

Job #2

1. Name and address of employer

_____

_____

2. Description of employer

_____

3. Job title

_____

4. Dates of employment (month and year)

_____

5. Reasons for leaving

_____

_____

6. Name and phone number of direct supervisor (will this person be a reference?)

_____

_____

7. What were your major accomplishments on the job?

_____

_____

_____

8. What were your major job responsibilities? In what types of tasks or activities were you typically engaged?

_____

_____

_____

9. What new knowledge or insights did you gain?

_____

_____

_____

10. What skills did you acquire or improve upon?

_____

_____

_____

Job #3

1. Name and address of employer

   _____

   _____

2. Description of employer

   _____

3. Job title

   _____

4. Dates of employment (month and year)

   _____

   _____

5. Reasons for leaving

   _____

   _____

6. Name and phone number of direct supervisor (will this person be a reference?)

   _____

   _____

7. What were your major accomplishments on the job?

   _____

   _____

   _____

8. What were your major job responsibilities? In what types of tasks or activities were you typically engaged?

   _____

   _____

   _____

9. What new knowledge or insights did you gain?

_____

_____

_____

10. What skills did you acquire or improve upon?

_____

_____

_____

Job #4

1. Name and address of employer

_____

_____

2. Description of employer

_____

3. Job title

_____

4. Dates of employment (month and year)

_____

5. Reasons for leaving

_____

_____

6. Name and phone number of direct supervisor (will this person be a reference?)

_____

_____

7. What were your major accomplishments on the job?

_____

_____

_____

8. What were your major job responsibilities? In what types of tasks or activities were you typically engaged?

_____

_____

_____

9. What new knowledge or insights did you gain?

_____

_____

_____

10. What skills did you acquire or improve upon?

_____

_____

_____

Job #5

1. Name and address of employer

_____

_____

2. Description of employer

_____

3. Job title

_____

4. Dates of employment (month and year)

_____

5. Reasons for leaving

_____

_____

6. Name and phone number of direct supervisor (will this person be a reference?)

_____

_____

7. What were your major accomplishments on the job?

_____

_____

_____

8. What were your major job responsibilities? In what types of tasks or activities were you typically engaged?

_____

_____

_____

9. What new knowledge or insights did you gain?

_____

_____

_____

10. What skills did you acquire or improve upon?

_____

_____

_____

Activities

List your participation in academic, professional, social, religious, political or charitable clubs or organizations (e.g., fraternities and sororities, Girl Scouts, Young Swinging Republicans, etc.). Also include your hobbies and leisure pursuits (e.g., collecting stamps, playing bass guitar, etc.).

Activity #1

1. Name of club, organization, or hobby

   _____

2. Your position or title. Were you elected to the position?

   _____

3. Dates of involvement

   _____

4. Principal activities of the club/organization

   _____

   _____

5. What did you accomplish while involved with this activity?

   _____

   _____

6. What were your major responsibilities as a member of this group?

   _____

   _____

7. What skills did you acquire or improve upon?

   _____

   _____

Activity #2

1. Name of club, organization, or hobby

_____

2. Your position or title. Were you elected to the position?

_____

3. Dates of involvement

_____

4. Principal activities of the club/organization

_____

_____

5. What did you accomplish while involved with this activity?

_____

_____

6. What were your major responsibilities as a member of this group?

_____

_____

7. What skills did you acquire or improve upon?

_____

_____

Activity #3

1. Name of club, organization, or hobby

_____

2. Your position or title. Were you elected to the position?

_____

3. Dates of involvement

_____

4. Principal activities of the club/organization

_____

_____

5. What did you accomplish while involved with this activity?

_____

_____

6. What were your major responsibilities as a member of this group?

_____

_____

7. What skills did you acquire or improve upon?

_____

_____

Activity #4

1. Name of club, organization, or hobby

_____

2. Your position or title. Were you elected to the position?

_____

3. Dates of involvement

_____

4. Principal activities of the club/organization

_____

_____

5. What did you accomplish while involved with this activity?

_____

_____

6. What were your major responsibilities as a member of this group?

_____

_____

7. What skills did you acquire or improve upon?

_____

_____

Activity #5

1. Name of club, organization, or hobby

_____

2. Your position or title. Were you elected to the position?

_____

3. Dates of involvement

_____

4. Principal activities of the club/organization

_____

_____

5. What did you accomplish while involved with this activity?

_____

_____

6. What were your major responsibilities as a member of this group?

_____

_____

7. What skills did you acquire or improve upon?

_____

_____

Skills

The focus here should be on what are often referred to as "hard" or "concrete" skills—meaning they can be observed and measured (e.g., computer skills, language skills, etc.). For each skill listed, indicate your level of competence (e.g., beginning, intermediate, advanced). The categories below are by no means exhaustive, so feel free to add others that seem appropriate.

1. Computers—software packages, hardware trouble-shooting, programming, familiarity with the Internet

2. Foreign Languages—specify whether you can write, read, speak, interpret, and/or translate. Also include your level of proficiency.

3. Math and Science—statistical analysis, research methodology, laboratory procedures

4. Business—cost accounting, financial analysis, economic forecasting

5. Arts—film editing, camera operation, set design, sewing, graphic design

6. Administrative—typing, switchboard, dictation, stenography

Now What Do I Do?

Congratulations! You now have all the raw material necessary—the facts of your life, so to speak—to create your masterpiece. The next step is to go out into the world and find a real life employment opportunity that intrigues you. It doesn't matter whether the position is currently available, as long as you know that it exists.

Now shift gears for a second and pretend that you're the employer and you need to fill this position. What skills and qualifications would you look for in an ideal candidate? Write these down in detail and rank them in order of importance. Now jump over to the other side of the desk and step back into your job hunting shoes. Compare the notes you just took with the information you've stored in your Qualifications Bank.

When you find a match between the skills, knowledge, and/ or experience you possess and what you would be seeking in an ideal candidate, do a little jig and make a big check mark next to the relevant Bank entry. After you've completed the entire review process, go back to each check mark (if you have none, you're either being too hard on yourself or you need to reevaluate your choice of jobs) and think about how you would transfer this information to your resume.

Why do this exercise? Because as a job hunter in what is essentially an employer's market, you need to make the best possible case for why someone should hire you. You need to tailor your resume as precisely as possible to the demands of the job in question. You must show the employer that you're not only a good candidate, but that you're the best one. Keep in mind that you may be one of 500 or more applicants vying for a single opening and that your resume may get only thirty seconds or less of the employer's time. There's very little margin for error. Your resume must be right on target.

WHICH FORMAT SHOULD YOU USE?

The format you select for your resume will dictate the manner and order in which your qualifications are presented on the printed page, and thus has some effect on how the reader will perceive your credentials. Although there is no one correct format, the approach you choose should make logical sense given your particular background and the sensibilities of the audience you're addressing. If you're applying for a job with a conservative accounting firm, then you'll obviously be best off sticking with a more traditional approach, whereas if you're shooting for a job in the music business, you can be much more creative. The truth is, however, that no matter what type of position you're applying for, your format choices are fairly limited. Essentially it comes down to a question of emphasis. Will you be better off stressing the various positions and titles you've held over time, the plethora of skills you've mastered, your most notable achievements, or some combination of the three? Now let's take a closer look at six different formats.

Reverse-Chronological

By far the most traditional and popular of all resume formats, and favored by nearly 80 percent of the employers we surveyed, the reverse-chronological format (see example 1) begins with one's most recent experience and works backward through time. This temporally-based approach appeals strongly to those who have a penchant for linear thinking—which unfortunately happens to be most of the people working in human resources these days. The reverse-chronological format not only provides the reader with a vivid picture of the applicant's career and academic progression over time, but also enables her to quickly determine where the applicant worked, when, for how long, and what she accomplished at each job.

While a good choice for the job hunter whose recent experience and training closely parallels the requirements of the position he is pursuing, the reverse-chronological approach doesn't work well for everybody. It's a poor choice if you have little or no relevant experience, a history of jumping from job to job, or significant gaps in your employment. Don't feel as though you must use this approach simply because it's so popular.

The Targeted Reverse-Chronological Format

This format (see example 2) is ideal for the person who has past experience relevant to her current job objective, but whose most recent experience is not within her targeted field. By creating targeted experience headings, this approach will enable you to emphasize your most relevant experience and avoid an unfavorable chronology.

For example, let's assume that you're seeking a job as a card dealer in Las Vegas. Although you have five years of Atlantic City dealing experience under your belt, for the last two years all you've dealt is burritos at Taco Bell. Using the targeted reverse-chronological format you would begin your resume with the category "Casino Experience," which will force the reader to focus on your most marketable experience as opposed to your most current experience.

The Skills-Based Format

The skills-based format (see example 3), commonly referred to as the "functional" approach, places the spotlight on what you can do, as opposed to where and when you did it. Your qualifications are grouped into experience categories (e.g., marketing, counseling, and research) the labels of which should jibe with the demands of the position for which you are applying.

The abilities you present on a skills-based resume are often extracted from a wide range of experiences, not just the workplace. While this format affords tremendous flexibility, it's not always well-received by employers (only 10 percent of those we surveyed listed the skills-based as their format of choice). Apparently, there's a perception among many employers that the candidate who resorts to using a skills-based resume must be trying to hide some awful skeleton in his closet. Funny thing, they're usually right. Nevertheless, a skills-based approach is still probably your best option if you have very limited direct experience in your chosen field, an inconsistent work history, or are trying to change careers.

Skills-Based Format with Employer Labels

In this format (see example 4) you use the standard skills-based approach, but also include the name of each employer beside your accomplishment descriptions. This technique enables the reader to more easily figure out each accomplishment that took place and where, and will help put many of the linear-thinking types at ease. The downside of this format, however, is that adding employer headings uses up valuable resume real estate and may force you to do some creative editing.

Reverse-Chronological with a Skills-Based Twist

This approach (see example 5) is especially effective if you want to draw the reader's attention to broad categories of strengths while staying within the safe confines of the reverse-chronological format. To do this, simply insert skills-based sidebars or subheadings into each job description. This will clue the employer in on what you believe to be your most marketable strengths. It will also lend clarity and structure to your job descriptions.

Accomplishments Resume

This format (see example 6) is tantamount to showing your prospective employer a highlight reel. It enables you to stress your most impressive accomplishments across the board and tends to work best with a unifying profile or objective at the top that guides the reader into your strengths. A bit of a wild card, this approach usually works best for experienced job hunters.

Resume Format Checklist		
Format	**Good choice if:**	**Poor choice if:/Cons**
Reverse-Chronological	Most recent experience is closely related to current objective You have a stable work history with no employment gaps Your career has progressed logically toward your current objective	You have an inconsistent work history You are trying to change careers Your most relevant experience is from a long time ago
Targeted Reverse-Chronological	Majority of your experience is in your chosen field, but your most relevant experience is not your most recent	Employer might be confused about where you are working currently
Skills-Based	You have a limited, irrelevant, or spotty work history You have acquired the bulk of your qualifications from non-professional experiences such as internships You have held several similar positions in which you performed the same tasks repeatedly	You are applying for a position with a very traditional employer. Many employers tend to be skeptical of this format, fearing that the job seeker is trying to hide something.
Skills-Based w/ Employer Labels	Skills-Based resume suits you but you want to make it clear where each of your accomplishments took place	Major drawback is that this approach takes up a lot of space and may force you to do some creative editing
Reverse-Chronological w/ Skills-Based Twist	You are a prime candidate for a Reverse-Chronological resume and your accomplishments fall neatly into discrete categories that are relevant to your prospective employer	This is a difficult resume to create and can backfire if the skills categories don't match up closely with the needs of your prospective employer
Accomplishment	Experienced job hunter with an impressive track record of achievements.	Difficult to pull off without a strong unifying theme. Profile or objective section must be well written.

PICK A FORMAT

Okay, no more dawdling—it's time for you to select a resume format. But don't worry, the choice you make isn't etched in stone—it can be changed at any time, and in any case should be constantly reevaluated as your employment situation shifts.

The best format for my resume is (check one):

Reverse-Chronological	_____
Targeted Reverse-Chronological	_____
Skills-based	_____
Skills-based with employer labels	_____
Reverse-Chronological with a skills-based twist	_____
Accomplishment-based	_____

Ms. Reverse-Chronological—1

Fifth Avenue • New York, NY 10028 • (212) 333–3333

Objective

Position as a staff nurse.

Education

Phillips School of Nursing, New York, NY
Associate in Applied Science Degree, Nursing, June 1997

Grade Point Average: 3.93

Honors:
- Dean's Honor List—all semesters
- Class Senator, 1993–1995
- Selected by faculty to participate in the Jacob's Perlow Hospice Conference on Nursing and Gerontology.
- Student representative—Faculty Curriculum Coordinating Committee

Experience

1995–Present
Beth Israel Medical Center, New York, NY
Student Nurse Extern, Emergency Department
- Assist RNs and physicians with providing emergency care to patients in a 32 bed Emergency Department.
- Perform EKG's, inserted foley catheters, administered glucose tests, and perform other procedures as requested under the supervision of a Registered Nurse.

1991–1994
Bud M. Weiser, M.D., New York, NY
Office Manager
- Liaison between doctor and patient.
- Coordinated hospital admissions and arranged outpatient testing.
- Handled insurance, billing, and correspondence. Diplomatically resolved payment disputes.

Community Service

- Burden Center for the Aging—provided companionship to the elderly. Planned and implemented special activities and outings.

Mr. Targeted Reverse-Chronological—2

25 Union Square • New York, NY 10003 • (212) 999-9999

Education   **New York University**, New York, NY
B.S., Accounting / Actuarial Science, May 1997
Honors   Stern Scholarship

Nassau Community College, Garden City, NY
A.A.S., Accounting, December 1993
Overall GPA: 3.88
Honors   Phi Theta Kappa
           National Honor Society

Business Experience

1992–1994   **H & R Block/VITA**, Valley Stream, NY
Tax Preparer
- Prepared individual tax returns for a diverse clientele.
- Acquired substantial knowledge of tax laws.

1989–1991   **Custodial Trust Company**, Princeton, NJ
Assistant Accountant
- Analyzed financial statements and reconciled general ledger accounts.
- Collaborated on designing a new billing system.
- Accurately maintained clients' accounts.
- Computed net equity reports and trading funds.

1989   **Whitehorse Savings and Loan**, Mercerville, NJ
Bank Teller
- Courteously satisfied customers' banking needs in this heavy volume, high pressure environment.

Additional Work Experience

1994–Present   **New York University**, New York, NY
Administrative Assistant
- Maintain various databases and oversee alumni billing.

Computer Skills

Proficient in Excel, Lotus 1-2-3, Q & A, FileMaker Pro 2.0, Paradox
Exposure to DOS, BMDP, Statistix, WordPerfect, Microsoft Word

Signor Skills-Based—3

West Street, Apt. A
Iowa City, IA 30024
(111) 777-7777

Education	**Bachelor of Arts, History,** May 1996
	University of Iowa, Iowa City, IA
	• Financed 50% of college expenses through various part-time and full-time positions.
Activities	• Rugby Club, President
	• Judicial Review Board, Member
	• Academic Search Committee, Member
Organizational Skills	• Managed annual Rugby Club budget of $50,000.
	• Coordinated fund-raisers, special events, and other activities, including the annual food drive to benefit St. John's Center.
Leadership Skills	• Provided general guidance and counseling to educationally and economically disadvantaged 14-17 year-olds.
	• Elected Rugby Club President for two consecutive years; increased club membership by over 75%.
Research Skills	• Conducted a comprehensive review and ideological analysis of Iowa's educational policies regarding minorities since 1954. Submitted report to the Iowa Education Department's Office of Equity and Access.
Employment History	
1995–Present	Youth Aide, Iowa Division for Youth
1994	Intern, Iowa Education Department
1992–1993	Various Positions, Mountain House

Skills-Based With Employer Labels—4

8th Street • San Diego, CA 11111 • (888) 888-8888

Education

University of California at San Diego, B.A., English, May 1995
Financed 100% of college education through full-time employment.

Writing/Editing Experience

Clearwater Revival
Write artist biographies for annual environmental festival; interview sloop club directors.

Women's Action Coalition
Assisted with writing a press release concerning the definition of women in the '90's.

Ultracomputer Research Laboratory
Assist Director with editing academic papers prior to journal publication.

Community Service

Grace Opportunity Project
Tutor fourth grade Latino students in reading, math, and writing.

UCSD AHANA Mentor
Mentored incoming NYU minority underclassmen to help ease their transition to college.

UCSD Higher Education Opportunities Program
Inform high school educators of higher education opportunities for their students.

Administration

Ultracomputer Research Laboratory
Maintain and format on-line resource library on UNIX system. Manage office operations.

Department of Human Services and Education/Resource Access Project
Played major role in assembling 600+ person conferences.

Computerland
Assisted Director of Finance in all phases of transition to on-line payroll system.

Professional Experience

Ultracomputer Research Laboratory, 1994–Present

Department of Human Services and Education, Resource Access Project, 1992–1993

Computerland, 1991

Skills

IBM: DBase IV, Lotus 1-2-3, WordPerfect, LAN • **Macintosh**: Microsoft Word

Reverse-Chronological With a Skills-Based Twist—5

Maple Street • Burlington, VT 00011 • (666) 666-6666

Summary

Extensive experience in a variety of non-profit organizations with proven ability in fundraising, marketing, public relations, program development, and counseling.

Education

University of Vermont, Burlington, VT
Masters of Social Work and Masters of Science in Non-Profit Management, May 1997

University of Maryland, College Park, MD
Bachelor of Science, Business and Marketing, Cum Laude, December 1986

Non-profit Experience

Founder, B.A.G.A.L., Brattleboro, VT   1993–1995
Marketing/Fundraising

Initiated and implemented various development activities including special events, direct mail, advertising sales, and community solicitation. Increased membership by 200%.

Public Relations
Established, developed, and maintained positive working relationships with various community organizations resulting in increased public awareness of and support for the organization. Designed promotional materials. Published a statewide newsletter.

Consultant, Brattleboro AIDS Project, Brattleboro, VT   1991–1992

Public Relations/Fundraising
Enhanced public relations through expanded community outreach, increased media contact, and the redesign of promotional materials. Planned special events; raised funds through community solicitation, and the initiation of fee based services.

Program Development
Gathered and analyzed data on trends regarding the transmission of HIV/AIDS. Developed and implemented community AIDS educational campaigns.

Caseworker, The Brattleboro Retreat, Brattleboro, VT   1990–1991

Counseling
Developed and coordinated treatment plans as part of a multi-disciplinary team. Direct clinical experience with a diverse caseload of patients in recovery from substance abuse.

Program Development
Designed and implemented Stress Reduction and Journal Writing programs for patients.

Additional Experience

Marketing Assistant, Patriot Bank   1987–1990

Joe Accomplishment—6   305 Commerce St., #5, Juno, AK 04101• 222.888.7777

Profile

- Experienced writer, researcher, and editor dedicated to creating information products (print/CD-ROM/on-line) that provide readers with reliable and accessible data.

Notable Achievements & Experience

- Compiled, edited, and published *The 1996–1997 Anchorage Dining Guide.* In charge of marketing, publicity, and distribution. Retail accounts include Borders, Waldenbooks, Barnes & Noble, and Bookland.   1996–present
- Author, *Eskimo Notes,* and Co-author, *Survival Smart* —Big House/Ivy Review   1997
- Content provider, *Career Toolbox* CD-ROM and Website—Chivas Regal   1997
- Author, *Trashproof Living*—Big House/The Ivy Review   1996
- Author, *Guide to Writing an Effective Personal Ad*—Crane & Co. Inc.   1996
- Editorial assistant, World Cup '94 Press Guide—World Cup USA   1995
- Edited a Ph.D. dissertation concerning the history of soccer in Brazil   1995
- Photographer, *The Landmarks of New York II*—Harry N. Abrams, Inc.   1995
- Career Resource Center Manager, New York University Career Services. In charge of acquisitions and cataloging; liaison to publishers   1993–1994
- Co-editor, *Career Guidebook*—New York University Career Services   1992–1994
- Freelance Fact Checker—*Avenue Magazine*   1991
- Author, *The Hypocrisy of Big-Time College Athletics for Men, Leisure Information Quarterly*   1990
- Sportswriter, *The Cavalier Daily*—University of Virginia. Covered soccer, wrestling, football, and cross-country.   1987

Education

Master of Arts, Sociology—New York University, New York, NY   1988–1990
Bachelor of Arts, History—University of Virginia, Charlottesville, VA   1983–1987

Computer Skills

Macintosh: Familiar with Microsoft Word and ClarisWorks; some knowledge of Pagemaker, Quickbooks, Quicken, Filemaker, Photoshop, and SYSTAT; frequently surf the Internet.

Employment Highlights

Freelance Writer, Counselor, Photographer—New York, NY & Portland, ME   1994–present
New York University Career Services, Career Counselor—New York, NY   1992–1994
The Vera Institute of Justice, Research Assistant—New York, NY   1990–1991
New York County District Attorney, Trial Prep Assistant—New York, NY   1987–1988

Learning
Resume-ese

If you're a budding Shakespeare or Alice Walker, I'm afraid you'll
have to keep your creative talent under wraps while writing
your resume. Interestingly, it's often the best writers who have
the most difficulty putting their resumes together. What you're
aiming for is clarity, conciseness, and punch, not Pulitzer
Prize-caliber prose. Write in the active voice in a straightfor-
ward style, keep your sentences short and to the point, and
you'll be fine.

Get rid of any words that don't elucidate the meaning you're
trying to convey or contribute in some way to your market-
ability. Avoid using personal pronouns, cryptic abbreviations,
helping and being verbs, and unnecessary articles. Basically,
you need to put a vice grip on your language and squeeze it as
tight as you can.

To maintain the reader's interest, vary your language as much as possible. We can't tell you how many millions of resumes contain job descriptions which begin with the phrase "responsibilities include." That's a real yawner. Instead, launch your resume statements with a power verb (e.g., improved, increased, and attained). A list of these verbs appears on pages 42–50. If you find that your language is getting repetitious, just consult your handy thesaurus to bail you out.

The words you use on your resume can instantly make or break your credibility with your prospective employer. It's okay to include commonly used buzzwords that demonstrate to your reader you know the lingo of your field. But don't get too carried away with highfalutin language. Remember that the first person who reviews your resume may be a human resources assistant who hasn't the foggiest idea what a "galactotropicoccus stethnorameter" is. Save the big words for the interview with the bigwigs.

 Perhaps most importantly, you need your descriptions to emphasize results and accomplishments. Employers don't just want to know what you were responsible for, they want to know what you achieved, and what, if any, effect your achievements had on your company's bottom line. One simple way to stress results is to use quantification. For example, instead of writing, "Raised funds for the Committee to End Suffering in Carmel," you could amend the statement to read, "Raised over $4,000,000 in a two-week period to benefit the Committee to End Suffering in Carmel." Using qualified statements is another way to spruce up your resume. Here the emphasis is on how *well* you performed a certain activity. For example, the relatively bland statement, "Resolved staff-management conflicts," could be rewritten as follows: "Resolved staff-management conflicts in a diplomatic and sensitive manner."

Power Verbs That Demonstrate Leadership, Decision Making, or Management Skills

Advocated door to door for the passage of "The Cats Are People Too Act."

Determined Karate Club policies and procedures regarding the admission of new members.

Directed a team of five oceanographers seeking the lost city of Atlantis.

Elected President of the City Council for three consecutive terms.

Enlisted the support of twenty volunteers to restore a community garden.

Formed a community task force to discuss how to revitalize the downtown business community.

Founded a volunteer organization dedicated to serving the needs of the homeless.

Governed the University Senate, adhering to the highest standards of honesty and integrity.

Hired a staff of fifteen phone interviewers for the alumni phone-a-thon.

Instituted "Carefree Fridays" to boost staff morale.

Led international visitors on a walking tour of Seattle's coffee bars.

Managed an exclusive fitness center catering to retired professional athletes.

Moderated a panel discussion on the impact of nuclear proliferation.

Operated a successful computer graphics consulting firm for three years.

Oversaw the distribution of refreshments to more than 5,000 marathoners.

Pioneered the first-ever pro-groundhog movement.

Presided over monthly student council meetings.

Produced an instructional video for the local Emergency Medical Service.

Recruited, hired, and trained twenty-five telephone interviewers.

Represented the student body on the Faculty Recruitment Coordinating Committee.

Spearheaded efforts to ban the use of animals in laboratory experiments.

Sponsored a bill to make all tuition benefits tax-exempt.

Staged a concert to benefit the victims of Hurricane Bill.

Started a campus-based travel agency to serve the university community.

Supervised twelve management trainees.

Power Verbs That Demonstrate Administrative, Organizational, and Follow-Through Skills

Arranged transportation to and from conference site for over 100 visiting scholars.

Assembled press kits and promotional packages for national rock 'n' roll tours.

Collected delinquent payments from patients with Delay Syndrome.

Coordinated seating arrangements at fashion shows for media and retailers.

Catalogued the private art collection of David Byrne.

Distributed a weekly newsletter to 4,000 subscribers.

Disseminated pamphlets on HIV to homeless streetwalkers.

Executed stock and option orders issued by retail brokers.

Formalized application procedures for the Alumni Mentor Program.

Implemented a computerized registration system.

Installed system software on over 250 computer stations.

Maintained a comprehensive log of acceptable sound takes.

Organized a ski trip to Utah during Winter Break.

Planned a twelve-part lecture series concerning international politics.

Prepared a guidebook listing low-cost mental health treatment centers throughout the city.

Processed over 100 financial-aid applications daily.

Routed over 500 calls daily to a staff of 25.

Recorded minutes at weekly staff meetings.

Reorganized the Career Resource Center collection based on the Holland codes.

Scheduled weekly social outings for nursing home residents.

Updated alumni mailing list for annual fundraising drive.

Power Verbs That Demonstrate Communication Skills

Apprised management of shifts in consumer buying patterns.

Answered caller's questions during an alternative music radio talk show.

Briefed reporters on recent developments in U.S. foreign policy toward Iraq.

Conducted fitness center tours for prospective clients.

Contacted magazine subscribers by phone to offer a special renewal rate.

Demonstrated how to use Word 7.0 to create an in-house newsletter in less than five years.

Drafted correspondence for senior management.

Educated parents of the physically challenged about the Americans with Disabilities Act.

Explained academic requirements to incoming freshmen at the College of Arts and Science.

Familiarized Cuban defectors with American customs and practices.

Handled phone requests for tickets to events at Foxboro Stadium.

Informed committee members of the various factors affecting the rise in violent crime.

Instructed a group of inner-city junior high students in the fundamentals of photography.

Introduced guest speakers during Career Week panel discussions.

Lectured American physicians about the benefits of Eastern healing practices.

Presented major selling points of the new swimwear collection to sales force.

Reported findings about commercial practices on the World Wide Web to the CEO.

Responded to phone inquiries regarding the admissions process.

Spoke at the AMA Conference on the relationship between diet and overall health.

Summarized the judicial board policies of fifteen liberal arts colleges.

Taught basic English to children of Mexican migrant workers.

Trained bartenders on how to properly mix Sex on the Beach.

Translated romance novels from English to Spanish.

Wrote a daily summary of New York Stock Exchange activity.

Power Verbs That Demonstrate Analytical or Research Skills

Analyzed blood samples to determine patients' cholesterol levels.

Assessed recovering clients' readiness to return to the workplace.

Audited financial records of the New York City Board of Education.

Compiled a critical bibliography of contemporary Brazilian music.

Consulted on the design of a multiplex cinema.

Discovered a new species of reptile in the Amazon.

Documented the history of soccer in Eastern Europe.

Edited book manuscripts for content and style.

Evaluated job readiness of newly arrived immigrants.

Examined supermarket poultry to determine salmonella bacteria levels.

Gathered data on property crime trends in the United States during the past ten years.

Identified elementary school students in need of remedial help in math and English.

Interpreted entertainment contracts and prepared contract amendments.

Interviewed varsity basketball players for a feature article in *The Targum*.

Researched the relationship between income level and political affiliation in Sweden.

Searched NHL archives for information on hockey in the United States. before 1920.

Surveyed over 2,000 Alabama residents to determine their opinions on TV violence.

Tested the effects of marijuana on short-term memory.

Power Verbs That Demonstrate the Ability to Create or Innovate

Authored two articles about society's preoccupation with psychic phenomena.

Conceived the international blockbuster film, *Transvestites in Turkey.*

Conceptualized a twelve-step program for chocolate addicts.

Created in-store displays utilizing glow-in-the-dark mannequins.

Composed a film score for a documentary on the Russian Revolution.

Designed a five-week intensive Spanish conversation course for hospital personnel.

Devised a direct marketing campaign for a nondairy frozen dessert.

Established long-term objectives for a national community service initiative.

Invented a solar powered light bulb capable of illuminating a 300-square-foot room.

Originated the "Fashion Compassion Ball," an annual fund-raiser for battered women.

Revolutionized the use of Styrofoam models in print advertising.

Power Verbs That Demonstrate Counseling, Helping, or Mediating Skills

Aided unemployed professionals with locating and securing part-time work.

Attended to the day-to-day needs of nursing home residents.

Assisted students with navigating through the career decision-making process.

Collaborated on the design of a new billing system.

Contributed to the development of a new, computerized tracking system.

Counseled college seniors regarding making the transition from school to work.

Comforted children suffering from various serious illnesses.

Facilitated the installation of a multimedia exhibit honoring female athletes.

Fostered the reconciliation between African American and Jewish residents in Crown Heights.

Guided high school students through the college application process.

Helped victims of child abuse regain their self-esteem.

Instilled confidence in individuals trying to overcome their fear of flying.

Mentored high school students considering careers in physical therapy.

Provided warmth and companionship to children suffering from leukemia.

Settled disagreements between landlords and tenants in an expedient and diplomatic manner.

Supported sales efforts of brokers by maintaining up-to-date client investment records.

Tutored elementary school students in basic math.

Treated patients with multiple psychological disorders.

Power Verbs That Demonstrate the Ability to Convince or Sell

Arbitrated a settlement between baseball team owners and players.

Convinced bar owner to introduce daily drink specials resulting in a 20 percent increase in profits.

Dissuaded union members from voting in favor of a walkout.

Marketed carpentry services via phone and direct mail.

Mediated conflicts between quarreling roommates.

Negotiated contracts on behalf of 1,200 union members.

Persuaded shoppers to sample perfumes and cologne.

Promoted long distance services to businesses in the New York metropolitan area.

Publicized film screenings via flyers, posters, and ads in the local paper.

Resolved disputes between management and staff concerning salary increases.

Sold advertising space to clothing retailers throughout California.

Secured new accounts by making in-person sales presentations.

Solicited alumni for contributions to build a new recreation center.

More Useful Power Verbs

Attained the level of black belt after only three months of intensive karate lessons.

Augmented sales by 25 percent through extensive phone follow-up.

Boosted net retail sales by 50 percent over the last quarter.

Broadened awareness of Middle Eastern politics through extensive travel.

Calculated daily shifts in foreign exchange rates.

Catered awards ceremonies for up to 3,000 attendees.

Decreased the average wait for course registration by 25 percent.

Developed a syllabus for a course on film noir.

Ensured customer accounts complied with Federal Reserve regulations.

Eliminated dangerous admission rites for newly accepted fraternity members.

Exceeded monthly sales quotas for two years in a row.

Excelled at providing professional, courteous, and efficient service.

Expanded retail operations to fifty sites nationwide.

Expedited the processing of transcript requests reducing waiting time by 50 percent.

Financed 75 percent of college education through full-time work.

Gained experience with a variety of desktop publishing programs.

Generated significant student interest in CIEE's work abroad programs.

Improved relations between staff and management by hosting monthly gripe sessions.

Increased paid membership by 200 percent within two years.

Launched a national public relations campaign for the Schick Tracer.

Mastered spoken Greek while traveling throughout Crete.

Published a monthly newsletter listing internship opportunities nationwide.

Reconciled out-of-balance expense accounts.

Reduced campus waste by introducing a dorm-based recycling plan.

Revamped the school library, making it accessible to those with limited mobility.

Revitalized the cheerleading squad by introducing contemporary costumes and dance routines.

Shopped retail establishments to determine current fashion trends.

Strengthened business relationships by providing superior customer service.

Supplemented lectures with role plays and interactive group exercises.

Utilized spreadsheet software to aid with line planning.

Building Your Resume Step by Step

The moment of truth has finally arrived. There is no longer any point in delaying the inevitable. You must sit down this instant and start writing your resume. Sure, it would be great to procrastinate for centuries, but the sooner you get cracking the faster you'll be able to land the job of your dreams. Before you get started you'll need to do the following:

1. find a specific opportunity for which you would like to submit your resume

2. compare the demands of the position you're investigating with the entries you've made in your Qualifications Bank

3. extract your most relevant qualifications from the Bank and list them on a piece of paper in priority order

4. choose a format for your resume (revisit pages 33–40)

5. sit down at the keyboard or grab a pad and pencil and get ready to start writing. Ideally, you should try to compose your resume with the help of a friend or someone who knows you well. You might even want to consider forming a resume-writing support group, the members of which would critique each other's resumes. At the very least, have two people you trust review your resume before you have it printed and sent out.

WHAT'S IN A NAME?

Your name belongs at the top of your resume, not the word "resume" or any other introduction. Your name will look best when centered or pulled out to the left hand margin. Make it larger than anything else on your resume and put it in bold type. If you're using 12-point type for the body of your text, then check out how your name looks at 16 or 18 points.

ADDRESS AND PHONE NUMBER

List your complete address and phone number. If you're living at a temporary address, indicate for how long that address will be valid and where you can be reached after that date. If you have a fax number and E-mail address, list those as well. While more and more employers are responding to inquiries by E-mail these days, most will contact you by phone—unless of course they have bad news, in which case they will generally reach you by snail mail.

You can list either your home phone number, your office number, or both. Do not list your office number, however, if you have limited privacy at work or if your boss doesn't know you're looking for another job. Otherwise, you may find yourself being scolded, or even worse, given the boot. And, while we're on the subject, it's generally not a good idea to print your resume at the office unless you want all your colleagues to know that you're looking for a new job.

The Profile

Just as the first thirty seconds of your meeting with a prospective employer sets the tone for the remainder of the interview, the first third of your resume often determines whether the rest of it even gets read. You need to make a strong positive impression from the start. One way to do this is to lead off with a profile or summary statement. The profile is particularly effective for the more experienced job hunter, although recent grads can also use it to their advantage. The profile statement serves as a coming attraction, prepping the reader for the feature presentation. It's a carefully crafted sound bite that proves to the employer in just a few lines that you're tuned in to his needs, and that you possess the qualifications he is seeking.

To know what these needs and qualifications are you have to have done your homework on your prospective employer. The rest is easy. Try to come up with two to four sentences or bulleted statements that communicate your most relevant credentials. Keep in mind, however, that you'll need to modify your summary depending on the requirements of each position for which you are applying.

Summary

> Five years of experience in advertising and public relations, with a strong track record in account management, direct mail, print production, and trafficking. Effective communicator with excellent organizational skills. Perform best under deadline pressure.

Profile

> - Four years experience in the food and beverage industry.
> - Excel at providing professional, courteous, and efficient service.
> - Substantial knowledge of haute cuisine and fine wines.

The Objective

Over 60 percent of the recruiters we surveyed favor the inclusion of an objective on the resume of recent college grads. Communispond Inc., a New York City-based consulting firm that trains executives in hiring skills, suggests that those who do the hiring make the first cut in the applicant pool by eliminating resumes without objectives. They reason that the job hunter who can state what they want in ten words or less is generally more career-oriented (*HRFocus*, January 1995).

The bottom line is that the inclusion of an objective makes the job of screening applicants' resumes a little easier by clueing the reader in from the start as to what the candidate's goal is. If you choose to include an objective, it should be focused and concise. A well-conceived objective demonstrates to your prospective employer that you not only know what you want in a job, but that you've also taken the time to learn what they want in a candidate. Although your objective should be focused, be careful not to make it too narrow, or else you run the risk of knocking yourself out of contention for jobs for which you might want to be considered.

OBJECTIVE
Position as a systems analyst in a UNIX environment.

OBJECTIVE   Paralegal position which requires expertise in legal research, Trusts and Estates, and Patent Law, as well as knowledge of Lexis and Westlaw.

EDUCATION

If you are a recent graduate, this section will be a major selling point and should be placed at the top of your resume, just below your objective or summary statement. However, if you already have a great deal of professional experience in your field, then your education section would come after your experience category. If your degree is actually irrelevant to the field you are entering, or could in some way be considered a liability, then it would be wise to de-emphasize your education section.

The core of the education section consists of the name of the institution you attended, the city and state in which it's located, the name of the degree, diploma, or certificate you received, your field of study, and the month and year of your graduation. After you've been out of school a while, just listing the year of graduation is sufficient.

EDUCATION   Northwestern University, Evanston, IL
B.A., English, May 1996

Do I need to list my minor?

You certainly have the option of listing your minor, as well as any other additional concentration of course work provided that this information would be of interest to an employer.

Education

New York University, New York, NY
Bachelor of Arts, Anthropology, December 1995
Minor: Sociology
Additional concentration in European History

I paid for college, not my folks. How can I get this point across on my resume?

Those of you who financed all or part of your education can add a line to convey this fact, such as, "financed 75 percent of college expenses through part-time work as a waiter, bartender, and messenger." This demonstrates to employers that you 're multidimensional and have a strong work ethic.

EDUCATION   Emory University, Atlanta, GA
Bachelor of Arts, Anthropology, December 1996
* Financed 75% of college costs. Worked an average of 25 hours per
week while carrying a full course load.

Does it matter in which order I put my degree and the name of my school?

The order in which you list your school and degree depends on what makes you most marketable. If merely uttering the name of the institution from which you graduated seems to generate "oohs" and "aahs" from your listeners then it would be wise to list the name of the institution first. On the other hand, if you received a degree which is in very high demand, such as a Masters in Occupational Therapy, then by all means list your degree first. If you went to a no-name school and received a no-name degree or attended a big name school and earned a big name degree, then it really doesn't matter which you list first. Once you've selected the ordering sequence that best fits your situation, you must remain consistent throughout the rest of your education section.

What should I do if I hold more than one degree?

If you're listing more than one degree, begin with the one that is most relevant to your objective. There's no law that says you must list your degrees in chronological order. And if you hold a prior degree that you feel is irrelevant or detrimental, then you have every right to leave it out. For those of you pursuing a graduate degree, it's usually a good idea to indicate your thesis or dissertation topic if you have one, and to include a brief statement describing your research or hypothesis.

EDUCATION   University of Virginia, Charlottesville, VA
Master of Arts, Sociology, May 1996
Thesis Topic: The Effects of Teacher's Expectations on Student
Performance in Elementary School

Princeton University, Princeton, NJ
Bachelor of Arts, Sociology, May 1994

Should I list my study abroad program?

Increasingly, many American organizations are considering it an asset for their employees to be globally minded and multilingual. They want workers who are sensitive to other cultures and adaptable to new environments. Studying abroad or participating in an international exchange program demonstrates to employers that you are interested in becoming more aware of the world around you. If you have participated in international activities, make sure that you describe them on your resume.

EDUCATION   Boston University, Boston, MA
B.A., Political Science, May 1996

BMT, Jerusalem, Israel, Junior Year Abroad, 1994 - 1995
Gained a deep appreciation for Israeli culture and history through a
mixture of formal education and extensive travel. Spent six months living
and working on a kibbutz.

Should I list my GPA?

Nearly three quarters of the hiring professionals we surveyed encouraged recent grads to list their GPA on their resume. Why such a high percentage? Because for many industries, recruiters are looking for an easy way to screen out the hordes of applicants that are knocking down their doors. Establishing a GPA cutoff is a convenient way to quickly trim down the applicant pool. GPA, however, is much less of an issue for grads who have been out of school more than a year, as well as for grads who are pursuing certain fields such as social service, where little emphasis is placed on grades.

Our opinion is that if you're a very recent grad, and you believe GPA is relevant to your field, and yours happens to be high—3.3 or above—then go ahead and list it. As an alternative you could list your academic honors or awards (e.g., Dean's List, Phi Beta Kappa) which in a more subtle manner indicate you have achieved high grades. If you're going to include your GPA, list whichever is the most impressive—overall, major, or minor.

EDUCATION   **University of Virginia**, Charlottesville, VA
Bachelor of Arts, History, May 1996
Overall GPA: 3.4

What should I do with my honors and awards?

Honors and awards tend to go over well with employers since, having been conferred by a third party, they are viewed as a relatively objective indicator of your abilities and achievements. When listing honors and awards, try to stress those that are most relevant to the job for which you are applying. Keep your list short, and make sure you describe the honor or award if it's not self-explanatory.

EDUCATION   New York University, New York, NY
B.S., Accounting / Actuarial Science, May 1996

Honors: *Racoosin Scholar*—participate in annual overseas excursions, attend guest
lectures, coordinate annual community service projects.
Dean's List (four semesters)
National Honor Society

What about relevant course work?

It won't hurt to mention a few of the classes you've taken that are particularly relevant to your career objective. Prioritize your list of classes in order of their relevance to the employer. Stick to listing classes in which you've performed well, and which are not typical requirements for your major. If you've taken introductory, intermediate, and advanced courses in the same subject area, only list the advanced courses, as it will be assumed that you took the prerequisites. Describe distinctive class accomplishments in the same way that you would describe achievements on the job.

EDUCATION
> Bachelor of Science, Mechanical Engineering, May 1994
> University of the Philippines, Manila

RELEVANT COURSES
> Machine Design—Constructed paper bridges capable of supporting 25 pounds.
> Turbo Pascal—Wrote a computer program to calculate the dollar's equivalent in 15 foreign currencies.

EXPERIENCE

The experience section is the heart and soul of your resume. Through it you are attempting to answer the employer's question, "If I hire you today what can you do for me tomorrow?" To do this adequately you'll need to offer concrete examples of your skills, and how you've used them to solve specific problems. Before you begin to write, arrange your accomplishments in order of how relevant they are to your target employer.

Use the power verbs we introduced earlier to give your prose a little bite. When appropriate, try to quantify or qualify your accomplishments and responsibilities. Keep your descriptions brief and to the point. There's no need to burden the reader with superfluous details. These can always be explained during the interview.

As you write your descriptions consider the following questions:

What did you accomplish or achieve at each position?

As has already been mentioned ad nauseam, employers are looking for results. They also want to get a sense of whether you take the initiative, or just do what you're told. This is the place to show them that you're a go-getter. If you're drawing blanks trying to answer the question above, ask yourself the following: What distinguishes you from your colleagues? Are you consistently praised by your boss for the way you perform certain tasks? Do your coworkers ask for your advice or opinion about how to carry out certain projects? Have you been designated to train new employees in certain procedures? Have you made any recommendations to your boss that have been put into use? Have any of your ideas regarding policy or procedure been implemented?

What were your major job responsibilities?

In other words what did you do all day long and more importantly, how well did you do it? Again, make sure you emphasize those skills and abilities that you would like to use in your next position and that would be of greatest interest to your target employer.

What new skills or knowledge did you acquire on the job?

This question is particularly relevant for those of you trying to describe an internship or volunteer experience in which you basically played the role of apprentice and were given few, if any, major job responsibilities. Try to communicate how you developed certain new abilities, improved others, and expanded your knowledge of the field by attending staff meetings, observing experienced pros at work, and providing administrative and technical support to staff, management, and executives.

What qualifies as legitimate experience?

Just about anything. You can include full-time, part-time, and seasonal paid employment, volunteer work, internships, consulting, freelancing, military service, raising children, globetrotting, and extracurricular activities. The issue is not so much whether you were paid, but rather what you accomplished through your efforts.

How should I handle odd jobs?

If you held a variety of odd jobs that you feel are worth mentioning but don't really require individual descriptions, you could lump them all together under one heading such as "Additional Experience," or "Other Experience." If space is an issue, this can help you save room on your resume for more important information. At the same time you will still be demonstrating to your prospective employer that you have been exposed to a wide range of employment experiences.

ADDITIONAL EXPERIENCE

1993–Present   Held a variety of positions while attending school part-time including waitress, word processor, caterer, and entertainer at children's parties.

What information am I required to include in my experience section?

At the bare minimum you need to include the name of your employer, the employer's location, your job title, dates of employment, and a description of what you achieved. If you have space you might also want to include the name of the division or department you worked for within the organization, as well as a brief description of what the organization does, its size (number of employees), scope (international, national, or regional), and revenues or budget.

TO BULLET OR NOT TO BULLET?

Nearly three quarters of the employers we surveyed preferred applicants to "bullet" their job descriptions because bulleted statements are easier to read than paragraphs. The only downside of using bullets is that they take up more space than paragraphs and are not scanner friendly (more on this later). If you do use bullets, you might want to try saving space by grouping related accomplishments together instead of listing each accomplishment on its own line.

Bullets organized by themes

Social Service Experience

Substance Abuse Counselor/HIV Program Coordinator,
1993–Present

Lafayette Medical Management, New York, NY

- Manage a caseload of 70 clients currently on methadone maintenance. Conduct intake interviews with newly accepted program participants. Provide individual and group counseling focusing on issues such as goal setting, employment, education, nutrition, health care, and hygiene. Monitor the results of weekly toxicological/urine profiles.

- Created the HIV Counseling Program which services over 200 participants. Coordinate weekly rap sessions; arrange guest lectures and staff training; organize various group activities; distribute condoms and safe sex literature; and conduct pre- and post-HIV test counseling. Supervise two program assistants.

Which comes first—my job title or the name of my employer?

The answer depends on which piece of information you believe will have the most positive impact. If you worked at a well-known organization as a peon, you're best off listing the organization first. On the other hand, if you were a VP at an unknown company, go with your title first. Unfortunately, once you've selected the "title/job" sequence for your first job, you'll have to stay consistent with that sequence throughout the remainder of your resume.

Do I really have to include my dates of employment?

Listing dates is a regrettable necessity unless you want to make it obvious that you're trying to hide something. Many recruiters we've spoken with say that dates are the first thing they look for. Nevertheless, you still have some leeway in terms of how conspicuous you want the dates to appear. If your career progression has been logical and steady, and you have no major gaps in your experience, then you can list your dates of employment in a prominent location. However, if you've had a series of short-term jobs, taken time off to learn windsurfing, or been out of the workforce for a long time, then dates become your enemy and your task is to de-emphasize them.

Although it's quite common to list the month and year of one's starting and ending employment dates, at times it's more advantageous to list only the year. For the sake of argument let's say that you started working at Taco Bell in June of 1995 and left your job in February of 1996. In July, you started a new job at Banana Republic where you are still employed. By using the "year only method," the five month gap will vanish as your resume will reflect that you were at Taco Bell from 1995–1996 and at the Banana Republic from 1996–present.

What if I have no professional experience?

Not to worry. Well, at least don't panic. Remember that internships, volunteer work, extracurricular activities, and basic life experiences such as raising a family, taking care of parents, maintaining a home, etcetera, can easily take up the slack. You can also fill the void by placing a heavier stress on your education section. However, if you're currently a student and have limited work experience, no matter how high your grades our advice is to start getting involved outside the ivory tower if you hope to be able to compete for jobs with your peers.

ACTIVITIES

Here's a chance for all you current students and recent graduates to show your prospective employer that college means more to you than just books and beer. This is an opportunity to demonstrate that you've had a well-rounded college experience, enhanced by involvement in a variety of school and community clubs, organizations, and athletics. By mentioning your extracurriculars, you convey that you have developed certain abilities and personal qualities that will make you an asset to any organization.

If you choose to create a separate activities section, then you should describe each activity just as you would a job, focusing on accomplishments, results, and the acquisition and development of skills, especially those that are relevant to your job target. You should also list the name of the organization with which you were affiliated along with your title if you had one. Dates are not really necessary.

ACTIVITIES

Connections, Alumni Mentor Program
- Meet regularly with an alumnus to discuss business issues.

Society for Creative Anachronism, Treasurer
- Oversaw the club's annual budget of $5,000.

Science Fiction Club, Vice President
- Coordinate the publication of the club's annual magazine.

SKILLS

This section provides you with an opportunity to tell your prospective employer about your "hard" skills—the ones you've described for your Qualifications Bank. These include speaking a foreign language, programming a computer, utilizing various software packages, operating a video camera, etcetera. Even if you've already mentioned some of these skills in your position descriptions, the skills section offers a nice, neat summary where an employer can see the whole package at a quick glance. List your skills in order of their relevance to your target employer and qualify your level of proficiency for the skill listed (e.g., fluent in French or basic knowledge of C++).

SKILLS   Familiar with Microsoft Word and WordPerfect.
                  Speak conversational Italian.

INTERESTS

More than half of the employers we surveyed recommended that recent grads list interests on their resumes, particularly if they are either unique or relevant to the job for which the grad is applying. Others told us that they considered the interests section to be irrelevant and a waste of space. If you do choose to list your interests, be careful not to give the impression that they are what you live and die for—after all, you're applying for a job. And one final word of caution: stay away from controversial topics like religion and politics. Listing them will usually only get you into trouble.

What should I leave off my resume?

Don't list height and weight, references, race, ethnicity, political affiliation, marital status, the names and ages of your children or pets, or the reasons why you left each job. Also, don't staple a photo of yourself to your resume.

ADDITIONAL CATEGORIES

Professional affiliations or memberships

This category is generally most appropriate for folks who have already established themselves professionally and are active members of one or more professional associations (e.g., The American Psychological Association). Active is the operative word here, meaning that you attend conferences, workshops, and seminars, and possibly serve on one or more of an organization's committees. Including this category demonstrates that you are committed to your field and interested in developing professionally.

Professional Affiliations
   American Association for Counseling and Development, Treasurer
   Career Development Specialists' Network, Membership Coordinator
   Career Resource Mangers' Association, Member

Professional development/Continuing education

This is a perfect section in which to list all the workshops, seminars, and classes you've attended that were not part of your formal degree program. For example, if you were employed at a large organization perhaps you took advantage of training that was offered in areas like conflict resolution, creative problem solving, or crisis management. Or maybe you sought out adult education classes on your own to try and keep abreast of what's going on in your field. Whatever the case may be, the point is that you have taken the initiative to enrich yourself, acquire new skills, and build your knowledge base. Those are achievements worth mentioning.

When listing classes the main thing is to indicate the subject being studied. Where and when you took the class are less important. However, if the course was offered by a world-renowned expert or at a well-known institution, feel free to list this information.

Professional Development
   A Neurodevelopmental Approach to Baby Treatment (5 day course)
   Neurodevelopmental Treatment of Children with Cerebral Palsy (8 week course)
   Systems of Communication for the Person with Neuromuscular Disorders (weekend workshop taught by Professor Franz Frankenheimer)

Licenses/Certifications

This information is a must for the resumes of nurses, social workers, real estate brokers, stock brokers, guidance counselors, teachers, and a host of other professionals whose fields are strictly governed by licensure.

Licenses/Certificates

New York Gaming School, Certificate of Completion, 1980
New Jersey Gaming Commission, Key Casino Employee

Publications

If you're going after a job in academia, journalism, or publishing, including your publications on your resume is essential. Be selective, though, as you can always submit a complete list of your published work at the interview. Make sure to include the names of any coauthors, the title of the article or book, the name of the publication, the name of the publisher (for books only), and the date of publication.

Selected Publications

"Incorporating Video into the Curriculum: A Teacher's Perspective," *Video and Learning Newsletter,* Winter/Spring 1993.

"Literature Adds Up," a chapter within the book, *Fact or Fiction: Reading and Writing Across the Curriculum,* The International Reading Association, 1992.

"Falling in Love with the Subject—Romance in Education," *Holistic Education Review,* Spring 1991.

Exhibitions

This category is appropriate for fine and commercial artists who have shown their work at galleries, festivals, museums, and other exhibition spaces. As with everything else on your resume, lead with your strengths and be selective. Start off with your most impressive solo exhibitions and work back through your group exhibitions. Make sure you list the name and location of the exhibition space. You may also want to list the title and year of show, and the medium of the work. Also indicate under a separate subheading whether any of your work has been purchased for the permanent collection of a museum or private collector.

Solo Exhibitions

1993   Crawford and Sloan Gallery, New York, NY
        "Romantic Visions"

1992   Fotozeller, Berlin, Germany
        "Peace on Mars"

Military Service

While most employers recognize the positive aspects of military service, it's still your job to convince them why this experience will make you a better employee. Instead of just listing your rank, describe what you perceived to be your major accomplishments.

Military Service

1980–1984 Captain, Israeli Army—Oversaw the training and supervision of 50
           soldiers and 5 officers stationed near the Palestinian border.

Tips for Making Your Resume Beautiful

According to the employers we've spoken with, submitting a resume that looks unprofessional is one of the surest ways to eliminate yourself from contention for a job, regardless of how impressive your qualifications may be. Most unattractive resumes spend only a few seconds in an employer's hand before they are condemned to the recycling bin. Yet you would be amazed at the resumes we've seen with ketchup stains, chewed off corners, handwritten updates, and illegible print. Fortunately, designing an attractive, eye-catching resume is not an impossible task, even if you failed art in second grade. You will need certain tools at your disposal however, including a computer, word processing software, and a good printer.

Getting Marginalized

Margins serve two important functions. First, they act like a frame, providing a welcome border of white space around your text. Second, they serve as a built-in memo pad for employers, many of whom like to make notes directly on your resume. Set your margins at 1" on all four sides to start. If space becomes an issue you can shrink them down to 1/2", but any smaller and your page will start to look extremely cramped.

Typefaces

Your next step is to select a typeface, of which there are two basic kinds—serif (the letters have small finishing strokes as with the typeface you're currently reading) and sans serif (the letters have no finishing strokes)—with hundreds of variations of each. It's best to use no more than two typefaces on your resume—one serif typeface for the body of your resume, and if you wish, one sans-serif typeface for your name and category headings. When choosing a typeface, consider the following issues—readability, attractiveness, and appropriateness. Traditional favorites for the body of the resume include:

Times

Palatino

Garamond

Goudy

Good choices for your name and category headings are:

Helvetica

Futura

Gill Sans

Stay away from fancy scripts, decorative typefaces, or any other type that strains the eyes. After all, you're sending out a resume, not a wedding invitation.

What size type should I use?

Generally you'll want to go with 10- to 12-point type for the body of your text, 12 to 14 point for your category headings, and 16- to 18-point type for your name. A point is a unit of measurement used in typography—you don't need to know any more than that. The only way to really decide which point size is best for a given typeface is to print a few lines of text and take a gander. If the type is clear and easy to read it's probably fine.

This is Times 18 point

This is Times 14 point

This is Times 12 point

This is Times 10 point

LAYOUT

There are literally dozens of ways to lay out a resume and we're sorry to say that there's no clear-cut winner. There are, however, certain basic rules you should follow. Your layout should always be clear, logical, and easy to follow, with plenty of white space. Remember that most employers will be scanning your resume, not devouring it word for word. Because of this, make sure you're consistent in your layout. Place key information, such as category headings, titles, names, dates, etcetera, in a logical order. Your reader will not be patient if his eyes have to wander all over your resume in order to decipher your qualifications.

FINISHING YOUR STROKES

There are five main text embellishment techniques to consider: **bolding**, CAPITALIZING, • bulleting (you can substitute dashes, diamonds, boxes, arrows, checks, pointing hands, or asterisks for bullets), *italicizing*, and <u>ruled</u> lines. <u>Underlining</u> is basically a holdover from the days of typewriters and is now considered pretty much obsolete. The problem with underlining, as opposed to a ruled line, is that it tends to appear clumsy and slices through the descenders of certain lowercase letters. CAPITALIZING should be used sparingly, as capital letters take up significantly more space than lowercase letters and will leave you severely pressed for room. **Bolding** works especially well for items that require the most emphasis, such as your name and category headings. All of these techniques will add distinction and emphasis to your text in varying degrees, and will make it easier for your reader to zero in on key information. In general, we would suggest you avoid the use of dingbats and graphics that tend to appear too gimmicky.

PROOFREADING

This is perhaps the most crucial yet most overlooked component of the entire resume-writing process. Never send out a resume before you've had it carefully reviewed by at least a couple of sets of trusted eyes for typos, poor grammar, awkward or repetitive language, a misaligned layout, and other mistakes. There's no margin for error. You simply cannot afford to miss any mistakes. A single misspelled word could very possibly cost you an important opportunity.

THE PAPER CHASE

Picking out paper and envelopes can easily be an all-day affair considering the mind-boggling array of colors, shades, textures, and weights. Use paper that's 8.5" x 11" in size and with a weight of at least 24 pounds (sometimes referred to as 70 lb. text). If you're using a laser printer make sure that your paper is laser-friendly. Texture is really a personal choice, although some papers will hold ink better than others. If you have any doubts, ask your local paper dealer.

Stick with neutral colors—white, off-white, ivory, light beige, and pale gray are all perfectly acceptable. The advantage of white is that it reproduces well when being either faxed or photocopied, whereas colored paper tends to come out with a muddied look. Fluorescent green paper will defi nitely get you noticed but most likely in a negative way. Stay away from loud colors.

ALL THE NEWS THAT'S FIT TO PRINT

For the best resolution and quality, laser printing is the only way to go. If it's too costly for you to have all of your resumes laser printed, you could make photocopies, as you need them, from a laser printed original. Never print more resumes than you're ready to send out at one time. Fifteen is a reasonable number unless you are attending a mega-career fair or other special event where you expect to visit with a large number of prospective employers at one time.

ENVELOPES

Using envelopes that match your resume paper is a nice professional touch, but white envelopes will always do in a pinch. If you really want to impress your prospective employer, send your resume and cover letter in a large envelope (9" x 12" is a perfect size). By doing so, your resume will arrive flat, a definite advantage if it's going to be scanned into a database.

The down side of using a larger envelope is purely economic. Not only are the envelopes themselves more expensive, but they also currently require a minimum of eleven cents additional postage as compared with standard business envelopes. Always have your final package weighed (or pick up an inexpensive postal scale at your local office supply store) if you suspect that it might exceed the allowable weight for the postage you intend to use.

Whichever type of envelope you use, it's important that you print the recipient's address legibly and correctly, otherwise your resume may never reach its destination. The address can be typed, laser printed or hand written (provided you have good penmanship). Sometimes handwriting provides a welcome personal touch, and ensures that the contents do not fall into the junk mail recycling bin. Also, don't forget to include your return address on the envelope.

GETTING YOUR RESUME INTO THEIR HANDS

The only thing left to do is make sure your resume (and accompanying cover letter) reaches your prospective employer in a timely fashion. There are several ways to accomplish this—traditional mail, E-mail, fax, courier, and hand delivery. The method you select should really be contingent on a) how badly you want the job, b) how long the job was posted before you heard about it, c) how much of a rush the employer is in to fill the job, and d) the personality type of the prospective employer.

In most cases, if the position was advertised, the ad will state the preferred method of resume submission. Follow the directions. Usually employers will ask that you reply by regular mail. If time is truly of the essence, "snail mail" may be just a little too slow. Many employers wanted to fill their vacancies yesterday. For the ultimate in speed, faxing or E-mailing is the way to go, but call the organization first and find out if they will accept either. If so, terrific, but always send a hard copy through the mail just in case the fax comes out mangled or the E-mail gets lost in cyberspace. If the organization won't accept a fax or E-mail, and time is of the essence, you always have the option of sending your package via Federal Express, UPS, or some other courier service. The U.S. Postal Service's Priority Mail is another possibility and it happens to be one of the most economical options. True, overnighting a package is an expensive proposition, but in addition to getting your resume into your employers hands quickly, you will be sending a message that you want the job badly enough to spare no expense.

Another alternative, provided the employer is within close proximity, is delivering your package by hand. This approach has the added benefit of enabling you to get a peek at your potential place of employment, as well as providing an opportunity to see some of your prospective colleagues in action.

Resumes of the Electronic Age

8

When E-mailing your resume you no longer have to worry about picking out a beautiful typeface, fancy paper, matching envelopes, or eye-catching postage stamps. Instead, you have another whole set of headaches to contend with. For one thing, although you'll be creating your resume on your word processor, you'll be saving it and sending it in ASCII format, which is plainer than vanilla, so you'll have far fewer options for making your resume attractive than paper provides. Basically, your graphic enhancements are limited to all caps, asterisks, dashes, and whatever other basic symbols you have on your keyboard. Also, you'll have to be careful not to exceed the character limit per line which is imposed by your E-mail program (check he program for the exact number of characters; you can ex pect it to be close to sixty-five) or the text that you thought would fit on one line will actually wrap around to the next one.

Make sure that you have the correct E-mail address of the recipient or your mail will be bounced right back like a rubber check. And finally, just as we warned against using outrageous outgoing messages on your answering machine, don't get out of control with your user ID, which is the first part of your E-mail address. Better to pick something innocuous like your name rather than a racy moniker like "HotStuff."

WHAT SHOULD I DO IF MY RESUME IS BEING FED TO AN APPLICANT TRACKING SYSTEM (ATS)?

Today, many large organizations including AT&T, Microsoft, and Nike, are adopting computer-based applicant tracking systems to speed up the review of resumes of prospective employees. In a nutshell, these systems use a combination of scanners and Optical Character Recognition software to convert your resume into text which is then analyzed by Artificial Intelligence. Because a standardized summary of your qualifications is created by the computer, it really doesn't matter much how eloquently your resume is written. The resumes of all applicants will end up on a fairly level playing field.

If your goal is to climb the corporate ladder at a Fortune 500 company, the implications of the computer resume revolution are substantial. Computers don't read resumes the same way people do. They don't have the capacity to assume, interpret, or read between the lines. Computers can only respond to information for which humans have programmed them to look. If your resume mentions the skills and experience that the computer has been told to seek out, then you're still in the running. If not, you're out.

In all fairness though, applicant tracking systems offer some decided benefits to the candidate. For one thing, they significantly expand the number of opportunities for which you will be considered, since your resume is always "in play." Each time a recruiter goes to the well to find a qualified candidate, your name has a chance of coming up. Also, it's likely that your "scanned" resume will stay active in the recruitment system for years, meaning that even if you don't make the cut this time around you'll have an equally good chance down the road. And finally, when submitting a resume to an ATS you no longer have to be concerned with the "one page rule." A computer doesn't care whether your resume is one page or three pages, so you can go ahead and let it all hang out.

For your resume to have a fighting chance with an ATS it's crucial that you describe your experience and accomplishments using the same keywords that employers will use for their database searches. Try to anticipate what they might be looking for (e.g., a specialized degree, experience with a particular company, fluency in another language, etcetera). The keywords used in searches are typically nouns, not the power verbs that we discussed earlier. For example, an employer might search for such keywords as MBA, Java, Japanese, copywriter, or CPA. Feel free to include jargon and acronyms that are peculiar to your field, as these may very well match some of the chosen keywords.

In addition, according to Resumix, the creator of one of the most popular applicant tracking systems in the country, you should adhere to the following guidelines:

1. Place your resume in a large envelope so that it arrives flat. Don't fold or staple your resume.

2. Use white paper.

3. Keep your layout simple—no two column or newsletter approaches.

4. Since the computer assumes that the first item on the page is you, make sure your name is at the top by itself. Also, if your resume is longer than one page, place your name at the top of all subsequent pages.

5. Each phone number you list should be placed on a separate line.

6. Use type between 10 and 14 points (with the exception of Times 10 point which is too small).

7. Don't condense the spaces between letters.

8. Stick with basic typefaces such as Helvetica, Futura, Optima, Universe, Times, Palatino, New Century Schoolbook, and Courier.

9. Don't use italics, underlining, shadowing, or reverse print.
10. Avoid using brackets or parentheses.
11. Don't use graphics or shading.
12. Don't use horizontal or vertical lines, boxes, or borders.
13. Use standard category headings such as Experience and Education.
14. Don't fold your resume. Use a 9" x 12" envelope to ensure your resume arrives flat.
15. Don't use staples.
16. Laser print your resume.

What if I have to meet with a human?

The fact is that these days you really need to have two versions of your resume, one to feed to the ATS and a second designed solely for human eyes to bring with you to an employment interview.

Is it worth posting my resume on the net or subscribing to a resume database service?

Every day it seems as though there's a new site on the World Wide Web that enables you to post your resume for employers around the world to see. There's nothing wrong with checking out these sites, as most of them are free and frequently feature some type of "Resume Builder" program that allows you to quickly create a resume online. Unfortunately though, there still seems to be little evidence as to the effectiveness of these sites. A better bet is to search for the websites of organizations that appeal to you, since many of these include a job opportunities section. Frequently, an E-mail or regular mailing address where you can send your resume will be provided.

You might also want to check out some of the job hunting newsgroups that permit subscribers to post their resumes for what should be a receptive audience. Again we have no data to indicate how effective this approach is, however it can't hurt to give yourself maximum exposure to potential employers.

9

Sample Resumes

The following "real life" resumes have been selected for inclusion in this book because of their ability to effectively generate employment interviews. They all demonstrate the various principles that we have tried to illustrate here. Feel free to borrow from them to create your own resume. Pay careful attention to format, layout, design, and phrasing. The resumes have been arranged in alphabetical order by field for easy reference. They represent candidates of varied backgrounds and experience levels.

Office Management (Lane Ryan)

Lane Ryan
4 Ford Street • Boston, MA 11111 • (617) 555-5555

Objective

An office management position which will enable me to use my skills and experience in:

overseeing daily business operations
purchasing equipment and supplies

team-building
supervising, hiring, and training personnel

Computer Skills

Proficient on Macintosh and PC systems IBM PCs:
WordPerfect, Microsoft Word, Multimate, Filemaker Pro, Lotus 1-2-3, and Excel

Professional Experience

CMC Communications, Inc. • Boston, MA

Administrative Manager • 1995–present
Hire and train administrative/support staff. Achieved staffing goals by streamlining and integrating existing positions. Supervise staff; mediate grievances. Purchase office equipment and authorize purchase of supplies. Established new procedures for production billing to maximize efficiency and contain costs.

Executive Assistant • 1994–1995

Worked closely with the company President. Ran day-to-day office operations. Acted as liaison between employees and upper level management. Oversaw work flow of secretarial/clerical staff, ordering supplies and equipment.

Administrative Assistant, Traffic Department • 1993–1994
Handled placement of classified ads in addition to taking care of all general secretarial duties. Worked closely with clients and media.

Additional Experience

Held temporary positions as secretary, receptionist, and office manager for various companies including The Freedman Group, Inc. (advertising), Woodside Research Group (market research), and Backhouse Productions (music). (1992–1993)

Education

Northeastern University • Boston, MA
Bachelor of Arts, English • 1992

Community Service

Volunteer ESL Tutor, Boston Community Educational Center • 1992–present
Soup Kitchen Volunteer, St. Timothy's Cathedral • 1993–present

Insurance (Terry Thompson)

Terry Thompson
3 Village Drive • Portland, OR 00038 • 222-999-3333

Profile

- 10 years experience in the insurance industry with expertise in underwriting, product development, contract administration, sales, and marketing. Excel at new business development. Broad-based knowledge of Group Life, Health, and Disability products. Strong track record of securing new accounts and developing and maintaining positive business relationships with clients.

Professional Experience

UNUM • National Accounts Risk Manager   1996–present

- Underwrite $40,000,000+ of Group Life and Disability products for UNUM's largest group clients, each with over 5,000 members.
- Maintain existing accounts and develop new business throughout the United States. Conduct sales presentations for prospective clients.
- Negotiate and price contracts with prospective and existing clients, brokers, consultants, and in-house sales representatives.
- Collaborate with UNUM senior managers including actuaries, and product development and marketing executives to establish pricing and product strategy.

Account Manager, Life & Health   1995–1996

- In charge of underwriting and marketing Group Life products to clients with primarily between 1,000 and 5,000 employees.

Sales Representative   1994–1995

- Sold Group Life and Disability products throughout the West Texas region to employers ranging in size from 2 to 2,000 employees. Conducted sales presentations for clients and brokers. Traveled extensively. Developed relationships with the regional brokerage community. Maintained and managed UNUM's existing accounts in the West Texas region.

Account Manager, Group Disability   1993–1994

- In charge of underwriting Group Disability products for UNUM's largest sales office (New York) which met or exceeded sales goals of $12,000,000.

Account Manager, Life and Health   1992–1993

- Underwrote Group Life, Medical, and Short-term Disability products for UNUM's largest clients. Trained and mentored both new and veteran underwriters.

Flex Product Development Manager, Life and Health   1991–1992

- Conducted research and development on flexible benefits for both Group Life and Medical. Managed a staff of three product analysts.

Senior Underwriter   1990–1991

- Underwrote Group Life, Medical, and Short-term Disability products for UNUM's Chicago sales office.

State Mutual Life Insurance, Worcester, MA • Underwriter   1988–1990
Household Finance, Springfield, MA • Loan Officer   1987–1988

Education

University of Massachusetts • Bachelor of Arts, Economics, 1987

Counseling (Nada Kendra)

Nada Kendra
1011 Oak Street • Rochester, NY 11111 • (716) 555-5555

Objective   Position as a counselor in a group home for emotionally disturbed adolescents.

Education

Bachelor Of Science, Syracuse University, College for Human Development May 1997
Major: Child and Family Studies
Coursework included education, psychology, and family dynamics.

Counseling And Teaching Experience

Community Medical Center   Syracuse, NY
Child and Family Counselor   Spring 1996
- Interacted with children and parents while children waited for medical treatment.
- Modelled effective childcare techniques and provided feedback to parents regarding parenting behavior.
- Established on-going relationships with families.

Syracuse University Early Education Center   Syracuse, NY
Student Teacher   Spring 1995
- Designed and implemented instructional activities for children ages 3 to 6.
- Researched learning styles and cognitive development of children.
- Organized and supervised educational field trips.

Elizabeth M. Wall Nursery School   Syracuse, NY
Student Teacher   Fall 1994
- Coordinated and led educational activities for groups of four-year olds.
- Planned new activities daily to teach group interaction skills.

Additional Experience

Cosmetics 'R Us   Rochester, NY
Assistant to Director, Creative Services   1996 to present
- Assist art director in coordinating photo shoots.
- Created and organized filing system for Directors.
- Identify new products and displays by speaking with vendors.

Leigh Barrett Boutique   Rochester, NY
Sales Clerk   Summer 1989
- Created window displays and performed in-store merchandising.
- Assisted customers in selection of merchandise; maintained inventory.

United Jewish Appeal and American Red Cross, Volunteer

International Experience

Haved lived in Australia and London; travelled extensively throughout Europe

NEIL WITHERS

1878 Harmony Street • Chicago, IL 22229 • (888) 999–9555

PROFILE

- Five years experience in financial services with a solid track record in securities sales, account management, and customer service
- Proven ability to establish, develop, and maintain excellent business relationships with clients and co-workers.
- Strong negotiation, communication, managerial, and interpersonal skills.
- N.A.S.D. Registered Representative   Series 7 & 63.

FINANCE EXPERIENCE

Sales Assistant to the Vice President   1994–1996
Butcher & Singer, Chicago, IL

Prospected, secured, developed, and maintained individual accounts. Issued quotes and confirmed trades. Ensured compliance with SEC regulations.

Investor Services Representative   1993–1994
The Fundamental Service Corporation, New York, NY

Provided comprehensive account services to existing shareholders. Expanded client base and maintained contact with over 3,000 clients annually. Informed clients of current market trends and forecasts. Diplomatically handled and resolved client questions and requests, including registration changes and liquidations.

Handled all aspects of mutual fund transactions - processed trades, issued confirmations, and assisted with reconciliations.

Registered Representative   1992–1993
Blinder, Robinson, & Company, New York, NY

Opened over 50 new accounts in less than a year. Acquired substantial knowledge of a wide variety of investment vehicles. Provided quality customer support to high net worth clients.

ADDITIONAL EXPERIENCE

Licensed Real Estate Agent   1996–Present
Madison Estates & Properties, Inc., Chicago, IL

Negotiate commercial and residential real estate properties. Analyze sales and demographic data, and make projections based on findings.

Provide consultation to rental agents regarding advertising, marketing, negotiating, and closing transactions.

EDUCATION

Bachelor of Fine Arts, Brooklyn College, Brooklyn, NY

Film Production (Mary Baggio)

Mary Baggio

111 East 20th Street, #0
New York, NY 10000
(212) 222-8888

film/video experience

Production Coordinator, 1995–Present

Atlantic Motion Pictures, New York, NY

Coordinate shoots of commercials; ensure that crew has access to all necessary supplies and equipment; check for color consistency and image quality during supervised tape transfers; maintain videotape library; liaison to vendors; appeared as talent in NBC Late Night promo.

Production Assistant, 1994–1995

Broadcast Arts Productions, New York, NY

Coordinated live action shoots of commercials; organized animation cells to correspond with storyboards.

Production Coordinator, 1994

R. Greenberg, New York, NY

Served as on-stage talent coordinator in a series of consumer products commercials.

Videographer, 1993–Present

Freelance

Conceptualize, write, direct and shoot short videos.

additional experience

Assistant Copywriter, 1993

Mirabella Magazine, New York, NY

Created descriptions to accompany photographs of fashion accessories.

education

BFA, Painting, 1993

Miami University, Oxford, OH

skills

Rough cut editing of 3/4" video
Black & white photography
Experienced with a variety of video cameras
Microsoft Word for the Macintosh

Current College Student seeking internship (Victor Magritte)

Victor Magritte

Local Address (until 5/12/97)
75 Avenue D, #244
New York, NY 10000
(212) 999–5555

Permanent Address
6 Sun Avenue
Staten Island, NY 10000
(718) 444–3333

OBJECTIVE

Summer Internship in a law firm

EDUCATION

New York University, Stern School of Business, New York, NY
Bachelor of Science, Accounting, December 1997
Overall Grade Point Average: 3.5

Related Courses
Business Law
American Government
Principles of Political Science
Principles of Financial Accounting
Micro- and Macroeconomics
Introduction to Computers and Programming

Study Abroad
BMT, Jerusalem, Israel, 1993–1994
Gained a deep appreciation for Israeli culture and history through a balance of formal education and extensive travel.

EXPERIENCE

Summers '92 & '93
United Video & Electronics, Inc., *Sales Manager*
- Supervised a staff of 5 sales representatives.
- Oversaw entire business operation during owner's absence.
- Contacted wholesalers via phone to place orders.
- Matched incoming shipments against invoices and resolved discrepancies.
- Researched media options for advertising campaign.
- One of two employees entrusted to handle the cash register.

Summers '90 & '91
Camp Mesorah, *Waiter/Cook*
- Served up to four tables simultaneously during lunch and dinner.
- Prepared meals for up to 500 diners at a time.

ACTIVITIES

Investment Society, *Member*
- Participate in discussions concerning market trends, attend lectures, contributing writer to club newsletter.

SKILLS

Computers
Quattro Pro 5.0, DBase III+, WordPerfect 6.0 & 5.1, DOS, Pascal, Basic

Languages
Fluent in Hebrew

Cory Johnson

225 East Wolverine Street
Detroit, MI 00028
(305) 999-9999

Profile

- Experienced computer professional with a strong combination of sales, management, and technical ability. Substantial knowledge of UNIX/X Windows and PC/MS Windows environments, as well as numerous applications and programming languages. Extremely well-versed with current developments in the software market.

- Excel at conducting convincing product demonstrations and presentations for both managers and technical staff.

- Skilled at establishing, maintaining, and developing positive business relationships with a varied clientele.

- Extremely versatile, adaptable, and well-traveled; bi-lingual—English and Hebrew.

Experience

Technical Sales Associate • *Mercury Interactive Corp.*, Detroit, MI   1995–Present

- Solely responsible for running the New York office of this rapidly growing 200 employee international firm specializing in software testing. Initially hired as an Application Engineer; have played an instrumental role in the company's growth.

- In charge of all aspects of pre- and post-software sales including, identifying and securing new accounts, conducting sales presentations for senior executives, negotiating and closing sales of up to $100K, and ensuring that clients receive the highest quality customer service. Major clients include, AT&T, Bellcore, Lehman Brothers, Citibank, Chemical Bank, and Dow Jones.

- Frequently sent to company sites throughout the U.S., Canada, and Europe to assist clients with launching new products using Mercury's software. Develop and solidify client infrastructures and consult on the software development cycle.

Software Engineer • *Strauss & Strauss*, Ltd., Ann Arbor, MI   1994

- Developed software using Assembler and Pascal for machines involved in the production of integrated circuits.

Sales Representative • *Pentogram*, Cambridge, MA   1993

- Sold lamination materials to clients in the Boston area while completing college degree.

Education

Bachelor of Science, Computer Engineering   1992
Massachusetts Institute of Technology, Cambridge, MA

Broadcast Journalism (Mia Spoleto)

Mia Spoleto

22 Park West, Apt. F • Minneapolis, MN 10022 • (222) 111-3333

Summary

More than five years of major market experience in TV and radio as a producer, writer, and reporter. Competent at coordinating all elements of production in the face of deadline pressure and budgetary constraints. Write effective news stories, features, ledes, narrations, and continuity. Ability to match visuals with compelling narration and/or music. Background in print journalism.

Television Experience

Field Producer, *Atlantic Media*, Köln, Germany   1994–present
Developed and researched feature stories for European television.

- Coordinated U.S. production; hired crews, scouted locations, and booked talent.

News Writer, *Satellite News Channel*, *Group W/ABC*, Stamford, CT   1990
Wrote news and feature stories for national 24-hour cable television network.

- Conducted telephone interviews, supervised video editing, wrote news wrap-ups, cut reporter packages, and produced voice overs.

Radio Experience

Correspondent, *Inner City Broadcasting-WLIB AM / WBLS FM*, New York, NY   1993
Wrote and produced reports on national, international, and local political and governmental issues. Recommended and selected stories for coverage. Anchored live news updates on breaking stories.

- Produced the City Hall Report, a daily update of key issues in city government featuring interviews with major political figures.
- Produced and co-hosted, You and Your Health, a weekly half hour talk show; interviewed medical experts about nutrition, AIDS, preventive medicine, and other health topics.
- Coordinated coverage of the 1993 New York City mayoral election.

News Editor / Reporter, Pacifica Radio-WBAI FM, New York, NY   1991–1992
Produced and anchored the WBAI Evening News. Utilized enterprising, investigative, and planning skills to deliver comprehensive coverage of breaking news stories. Supervised and trained a staff of reporters.

- Coordinated coverage of the Democratic Convention and '92 presidential election.
- Hosted national programs on race relations, the environment, and women's issues.
- Produced arts and entertainment features .

Education

Master of Science, Broadcast Journalism, Columbia University • 1990

Bachelor of Fine Arts, Film and Television, New York University • 1988

Recent Graduate—Liberal Arts Major (Lianna Maria White)

Lianna Maria White
15 River Street, Apt. #3
Pittsburgh, PA 10000
(222) 555-5555

EDUCATION

Carnegie Mellon University, Pittsburgh, PA
Bachelor of Arts, Politics/History, May 1997

Minor: Spanish
Major GPA: 3.2
Honors: College of Arts and Science Scholarship

- Financed 50% of college costs through various part time jobs.

Relevant Courses

Power and Politics in America
International Politics
Comparative Politics

American Constitutional Law
Women in Law
United States History

EXPERIENCE

1996–Present

Carnegie Mellon University, Pittsburgh, PA
Admissions Ambassador

Conduct campus tours for up to 25 prospective students and their parents. Respond to phone inquiries regarding admissions and specific academic programs. Represent Carnegie Mellon at open houses and other special events. Provide administrative support within the Admissions Office.

Fall 1995

Investors Associates, Pittsburgh, PA
Sales Assistant

Supported sales efforts of brokers by maintaining up to date client records and daily logs of stock purchases and sales. Coordinated follow-up mailings to clients.

Summer 1994

Edward Isaacs & Company (CPA's), Pittsburgh, PA
Telemarketer
Laid the groundwork for the sale of financial software by convincing potential clients to register for a free evaluation of their computer systems. Heavy phone contact with high level executives. Maintained client leads via computer.

ACTIVITIES

Democratic Club—Organized and promoted club activities and events; assisted with voter registration drive.

Pre-Law Society, Member

ESL Tutor

SKILLS

Languages: Fluent in Spanish
Computers: Macintosh: Microsoft Works • IBM: WordPerfect 5.1

INTERESTS

International travel (have visited several countries in Central America and Europe), flute, art museums, ethnic fairs and festivals, Spanish literature, foreign films, African history

Sports Administration (Guy Parent)

Guy Parent

41 Hall Street • South Orange, NJ 00000 • 201 333-3333

Profile

15 years of sports management experience with proven ability in special events coordination, program development, marketing, and facilities management. M.A. in Sports Administration..

Sports Administration

Oversee operation of college recreation center. Manage student employees and union maintenance workers while catering to the needs of student athletes and facility members—Seton Hall University, South Orange, New Jersey.

Scheduled varsity and junior varsity sports for boys and girls high school including soccer, basketball, baseball and softball. In charge of selection of coaches, transportation arrangements, field acquisition and equipment purchasing—Berkeley Carroll Street School, Brooklyn, New York.

Administered staff of 30 employees at health club. Responsible for hiring, firing, scheduling and setting policies—Dearborn Racquet and Health Club.

Marketing/Special Events Experience

Produced and directed major school fund-raising event involving over 120 students, 50 parent volunteers and many local businesses—Marshall/Jefferson Schools PTA, Maplewood/South Orange.

Developed marketing strategy instrumental in conversion of racquet club to total health facility. Helped create radio spots, advertisements and press releases—Dearborn Racquet and Health Club, Dearborn, Michigan..

Staged Jump-a-thon in support of the American Heart Association, attracting major network TV coverage—The Cathedral School, New York City.

As VP of Promotions coordinated fund-raising events for the South Orange Public Library.

Work History

1995–present	**Facilities Manager**, Seton Hall University, South Orange, NJ
1994–present	**Instructor, Weekday Nursery School**, South Orange, NJ
1994–present	**Aerobics/Tennis Instructor**, 41 Sports Club, South Orange, NJ
1993–1994	**Athletic Director**, Berkeley Carroll Street School, Brooklyn, NY
1992–1993	**Assistant Manager**, Dearborn Racquet and Health Club, Dearborn, MI
1991–1992	**Physical Education Instructor**, Cathedral School, New York, NY

Education

M.A., Sports Administration, Wayne State University, Detroit, Michigan, 1993

B.Ed., Physical Education, McGill University, Montreal Canada, 1991

Athletic Accomplishments

McGill University—Goalie, Varsity Ice Hockey
Outstanding Woman Athlete in Education Faculty

About the Author

Since 1988, Tim Haft has helped thousands of job seekers from all walks of life and all corners of the globe to find meaningful and satisfying work, and in some cases just a plain old job. Mr. Haft is the author of *Trashproof Resumes* (The Princeton Review/Random House, 1995) and *Crane's Guide to Writing an Effective Resume* (Crane & Company, 1995) and is co-author of *Job Smart* (The Princeton Review/Random House, 1997). He is also a contributor to *The Career Toolbox*, an interactive CD for job hunters. Mr. Haft has served as a career counselor at New York University and the Fashion Institute of Technology, and has held roughly thirty-five other positions over the past fifteen years. He is currently Senior Editor at a national, nonprofit association that assists high school students with the transition to college. Tim holds a B.A. in history from the University of Virginia and an M.A. in Sociology from New York University.